Millionaire Habits: How to Use it to Change Your Life

Alex Pust

ISBN: 9781973139539

Table of Contents

Introduction

Many people have read books and attended seminars on how to become wealthy. Even friends have offered advice, yet for many of these people, they are still in the same position as when they started. Nothing has changed, and they inadvertently, have not become wealthy as they dreamed.

Once the initial boost and enthusiasm begin to wane, ordinary life begins to creep back in, and you do find yourself again at the start of your journey. There is one contributing factor that dictates this success, and it is what most people don't realize. We all have a financial plan in our mind, it is sort of like a money map, and if this is not set for success. It does not matter what you learn, what you know, or what you do, you will never achieve the success that you aim for.

Millionaires are no different from the rest of us, they only have good habits that drive them to their goals and ultimately, their success. In the pages of this book, we will see what causes us to have a money map that is not geared for success, from childhood influences and our self-destructive thoughts. We will learn how you can change these habits and replace them with beliefs, and practices that improve the way you will come to think of your success.

Included are strategies that you can use as a guide to increase your income and to help build and maintain your personal wealth.

Part one of this book looks at how each of us has been conditioned how to think and how to act when we deal with money. Here I'll show you four ways that everyone can revise their mental money map.

The later pages of the book show how successful people conduct themselves throughout their days, what they do and how they do it. These can be introduced into your life, and you too can adopt their way of thinking.

Most of what is written in this book have come from my own personal experiences. I used to be one of the people who had the wrong money map, and that I managed to change by following the very same principles. In my younger years, I was obsessed with becoming successful, the reason for this at the time was unclear. I wasn't sure if I wanted to be wealthy or to prove how good I was to my parents.

After a few, not so successful business start-ups and working my fingers to the bone. I began looking at why some people some of which I knew, were becoming successful, yet I was failing. Time and Time again.

After some very in-depth soul searching and self-realization. I took a long look at my beliefs. Even though I had done everything in my power to become successful, I could see, I had some worries about doing so. Many of these were insecurities of being a failure (I already had failed) or becoming successful, and then letting it all slip away and losing everything.

One day I had a meeting that was not purely by chance. A close family friend, a wealthy friend, noticed I was down in the dumps. After a few prying questions, he gave me some advice. I was sure it was going to be advice I had already heard, and I was ready to block my ears while he spoke. Within his first couple of sentences, he had sparked my interest.

He did rub it in slightly saying he had also been a disaster, I had failed, yet I didn't want to class myself as a disaster, not that early anyway.

He explained that if I was not doing so well, it was because of something I didn't know. I was dead sure, I knew everything. Until my father's friend spoke again.

"Do you know that rich people (millionaires) think in the same way as other rich people, which is different to regular people?" I hadn't ever thought about it. He went on to explain that these thoughts, or ways of thinking affect our actions and then lead us to our results.

His final statement was, that if I copied the thoughts of successful people, I could change my minds money map and become successful, as I had already tried (and failed)to be.

From this point, I started to research as much as I could about the mind, and how it is affected by these thoughts of "successful" people. I found it was true what my father's friend had told me.

From this point forward, I became aware of my thoughts and how they were holding me back. I also learned the very techniques and strategies I'll show you later.

I borrowed money to try once again, yet this time I would put all I learned into practice. I used what I had gained from modeling rich people in their thinking and business strategies. I found that thinking short-term leads to distractions from what appear to be excellent opportunities, or when things got difficult.

If I found myself thinking negatively, I consciously chose not to entertain these thoughts, as they were the ones that were holding me back on previous occasions.

To cut a long story short. All of the things I had learned and put into action worked. So much so, after two and a half years, I was able to sell my latest startup, and focus on refining the strategies I'm going to show you.

As you read further, this book is not just about learning more, it is about forgetting the way you have been thinking, and changing your mental outlook.

Chapter One: Your Personal Money Map

It is impossible not to have an opposite side of something. Hot and cold, black and white. There are many such examples of this, and money being one of them.

When we look at money, we would say it has an inner and an outer. The outer includes things such as money management, business management, and opportunities for investing. These strategies are essential.

We also have an inner which is as important. An example would be craftsmen, who have tools. Having the best tools is crucial, yet not as important as being the best craftsman, who can use his tools.

We have all heard the saying "being in the right place at the right time. We can take this further and say "we have to be the **'right'** person, in the right place at the right time."

We then move on to your own personal circumstances: Who are you? What are your beliefs? What habits and traits do you have? And how confident are you in yourself? There are more of these questions you can ask yourself, and one of the main ones being, Do you feel deep inside yourself you deserve success and wealth?

From answering these personal questions we ask ourselves, we find our character goes a long way in dictating the levels of our success.

Why your Money Map is Important.

We have all seen the people who have large amounts of money and then lose it, or they have a great business opportunity that does well, and then falls apart. It may appear that they have been a victim of bad luck, yet this is not the case. From the introduction, you can see it is more likely from the fact, they were not ready to receive this (success) on the inside. Their money map was not set out correctly.

Being ready to accept this sort of wealth is as important as the actual receipt of it. Many people though do not have this internal capacity of holding onto, let alone creating these vast amounts of money. They also don't have the resources to deal with the challenges that come with this situation.

A prime example being lottery winners. There are so many who have won a fortune, only to spend or lose it all, and return to a more comfortable level and financial status they can handle. At the other end of the scale we have the self-made millionaires, if they lose their wealth, it has been shown, within a short period of time, they can gain it all back, and in many cases, their wealth increases from the level they lost.

Each person has an inbuilt level of money that they are happy with. A vast amount of people have internal settings to earn thousands while some are set to making hundreds of thousands. We then have the people with super high settings of earning millions and billions.

Take a billionaire and ask them how they would feel about being a regular millionaire, they would not be happy or settle for that amount.

We also have the individuals whose money maps are set internally below zero. They have no idea why they have no money; while studies have shown, that around eighty percent of people never reach being financially free in a way that would make them happy. It is this eighty percent who also claim to never be thoroughly content.

Through peer pressure and social conditioning, many people become oblivious to all of this, and it is for this reason, they work and live on one superficial level which is based, on what they are able to see around them.

Look at the Roots.

If we base an example of fruits being our results. When we deem our fruits to be small, or there are not enough, we focus our attention on the fruits to make them better and bigger. If we stepped back and looked at what creates these fruits (our results), we would see that it's the seeds and the roots that govern the sort of fruits we gain.

Most of us miss this, as roots are invisible, we only focus on the visible. So, if we wish to change what we can see and become successful, we have to first change and nurture what we are unable to see.

When we go against this and just believe what we see, we are in fact going against the laws of nature. As humans, we were created by nature, so if we focus on our inner (invisible) self, we can have a life that flows naturally. If we don't, and we focus on what we can see, life can become much rougher and tougher.

Four Quadrants of Life

We are led to believe we live in one realm. Where in fact we live in four realms at the same time. These can be separated by the spiritual world, the mental world, the emotional world, and the physical world. It is this physical world that is a printout of the other three parts of the quadrant.

When we look at life regarding these four quadrants, we see the following. Money is only a result, as is wealth, this is also just a result. Even illness is just a result. We do live in a world that is controlled by cause and effect.

"Not having money is a problem." How many times have we heard that? What we should be looking at is, what is causing the lack of money; and that my friends are the real problems?

If we are having a rough time and our outer is having problems, these are only the "results" of what is happening underneath or inside. Our outside is a reflection of our inside, and to balance these, we need to work on the inside first.

Chapter Two: Enforcing Declarations

There are techniques that can help you to learn quicker and keep more information. These are "Accelerated" learning techniques. One of the main keys in these techniques is being involved. If you take the old saying, "what you hear, you forget; what you see, you'll remember, and what you do, you'll understand."

For this reason, I'll give you a task. At the end of every major part from this point forward, you put your hand on your heart and make a verbal (say out loud) declaration. Once you have done this, place an index finger on your brow and make another verbal (say out loud) declaration.

You might be asking, what are declarations? Declarations are positive statements you give to yourself. By saying it out loud you enforce the thought, which in time becomes a part of your subconscious (rather like a habit).

There is also the spiritual side of touching when you say your declaration out loud. The body is made from one energy, which flows in frequencies. Each declaration you speak out loud has its own frequency; and through touching, this energy vibrates through the cells of your body.

On some occasions, declarations become mixed up with affirmations, yet there is a slight difference between the two.

Affirmations are positive statements you are already achieving something toward reaching your goals.

Declarations are statements of intentions to take **official** particular courses of **action**.

Although quite similar, you better sticking with declarations as affirmations have one downfall. If you make an affirmation about something that is happening, and you don't reach your goal? Your inner voice will be telling you it is all a crock, and isn't true. Affirmations do work for some people and you are free to use them as you wish.

Declarations though don't state that anything is true. They state we have the sole intention of performing some action. Our minds can accept this more easily, as we have not physically done anything that can fail.

Declarations also become like an "official" statement by the speaking out loud and the touching of your heart and your head. Another crucial word taken from a declaration is "action." Without this, you would not take all the necessary actions to make all your intentions (goals) become a reality.

To enforce these declarations, you should spend a few minutes at the start and the end of each day performing them. One other item that can help enforce these is the use of a mirror. As you watch yourself performing your declarations, you will help to speed up the process of enforcing these.

It is at this point, you might be thinking, these can't work. I used to be of the same opinion, but as I mentioned. After two and a half years of doing everything in this book, I could sell off my business for quite a substantial amount.

Here is an example of a declaration. It covers what you want to do, as the whole aim is to be a millionaire. Is it not?

Example:

Hand on heart and say out loud.

"My inner being (world) creates my outer being (world).

Don't forget to touch your brow and say.

"I possess a millionaires mind."

What is your Money Map?

We all have these money maps or plans inside of us, and they are embedded deep in our subconscious. It is this that will dictate the level of success that you will achieve. Simply put, it is what is preset inside of you, or a way of being in relation to success and wealth (money).

From here there is a formula that has been created by some of the best known teachers in the human potential. Better known as the Process of Manifestation it goes as follows.

T + F + A = R

The principal meaning of this is:

Thoughts lead to feelings.

Feelings lead to Actions.

Actions lead to results.

All of these are included in your money map, and it is a combination of these that relate to your sub conscious thoughts of money.

You might ask how this becomes to be formed, yet the answer is rather simple. Your money map was programmed by information you received in your past, and importantly during your years as a child.

We often find for the majority of people the main contributors were Parents, Siblings or friends in a close circle. In an outer circle of influence are teachers, figures of authority, media and our culture.

Culture for one has a large bearing on people's money map. We know that some cultures think of money in a totally different way to another culture. When children are born, they have to be "taught" how to deal with money, it is not something that is passed down through birth.

This is the same for everyone where money is concerned, we have all been taught of how to act and how to think about money. These teachings quickly become our conditioning, and from here, we have automatic responses that remain with us throughout our lives.

The good news is, we are getting to the point where you find, you can intervene and change your money map. All of our thoughts come from our earlier conditioning, these in turn lead us to our actions. So, no matter what thoughts we have, they all stem from conditioning and programming we received when we were younger.

We can now revise the Process of Manifestation into the following:

P + T + F + A = R

You can see it is the programming that gives you your thoughts before your feelings and actions.

Chapter Three: Conditioning

Before we can think about changing our money map, we have to understand what led to our conditioning. This basically comes from three main areas which are found in every single area of life, money included.

Modeling

This is one of the ways in which we are conditioned as children, and it has a direct way of relating to how are parents were with money as we were growing up. When we saw how they handled money, if they were savers or spenders or even conservative or risk takers?

There are lots of questions you can ask of how your parents dealt with money, and unfortunately we learn most of our things from modeling our parents. In the beginning I was following my father's up and down moments, and this was one of the first things I realized that was causing me to fail. The moods and the self-doubt crept in a little too often.

We can see children who are raised in poorer families who use their situation as motivation to improve their situation. In one way this is good, yet in another, they might have worked hard and made a fortune but they seldom become happy with their success.

There is one reason that leads to this, as children they had their buttons pushed by their parents. Storming to the bedroom and screaming "I'll never be poor." Reflects back on angry rebellious times which gets carried forward to their motivation.

The resulting subconscious kicks in, and these people make bad decisions or overspend. Their wealth dwindles until they revert back to a level they are comfortable and have no anger building inside of them. This might sound as if it is not possible to do, but all of this happens on a subconscious level.

When we begin changing our money map, we have to be sure our motivation is pure and not one that stems from anger or a need to prove how good you are. If these are influencing factors, you will find, you will never be truly happy.

Tip: If you are ever asked the motivation for becoming successful and rich, and you give security as motivation (as most people do). You will find security and fear have the same motivation. Money will never resolve fear, so money will never solve security or fear, as these are not the problems.

The more money we have, the types of fears and insecurities we have changes. When we break the links of anger and fear, or the need to prove yourself as motivation, we can re-build new links of joy, contribution and a sense of purpose.

Changing Your Modeling.

Being Aware - Sit down for a few minutes, and look back how your parents were with money and wealth. On a piece of paper write down how you follow the way they were or how you are the opposite of how they acted.

Understanding - Write down how the modeling you received from your parents, has affected your financial life and situation.

Disassociation - Now you should be clearly able to see that this modeling is only what you learned as a child. You will also see, this is not the real you, now this is in the open, you will see you have a choice where you can be different.

State your Declaration

Hand on heart and say out loud.

My modeling around money was my parent's way. I choose my way

Now touch your brow.

I possess the mind of a millionaire.

Incidents

Specific incidents will also influence us in the way we are conditioned. Was there anything specific you experienced when around wealthy people? The experiences we have, are enforced as it is what we have done, our beliefs become shaped and these illusions are what you will be ultimately living by.

If you experience anything related to money as a child and the resulting situation is traumatic, this feeling will be with you when you have money. It is from these traumatic experiences that as adults, we subconsciously get rid of our money as we associate it with the feelings of pain, anger or loss etc.

There is an aside to these incidents. If you are in a relationship, you have to consider your partners money map. They might have incidents of happiness or pain, and if you have an attitude for saving, there could be clashes. These clashes just so happen to be the number one cause for relationship break-ups.

Tip: Choose understanding over becoming upset or angry with your partner. Find out what is important to them when they relate to money. Do they have any deep fears, or what is their motivation? **As mentioned earlier look at the Roots not the fruits.**

Changing your Incidents

Sit down with your partner and discuss both of your histories relating to money. At the same time, look for what your partner really thinks of money and what it means to them. From this you can start to identify each other's money map, and what is causing the arguments.

You can both discuss as a partnership what you want, agree on goals and your attitudes towards your success and money. These should be written down along with the actions you both agree to do to reach your goals. Post these in a visible place and should the occasion occur, give your partner a gentle nudge they are straying away from their commitment.

Time for a declaration.

I banish unsupportive money experiences from my past. I will create a new wealthy future.

Now touch your brow.

I possess the mind of a millionaire.

Verbal Programming

This looks back to what you heard as a child regarding money and wealth. It is obvious you heard many phrases during these times:

Money is the root of all evil?

Save your money for a rainy day.

Money doesn't grow on trees.

Am I made of Money?

There are many more sayings, all of which lean one way or the other. The one thing with these sayings is, they become rooted in your subconscious and remain with you throughout your life. If you had heard that rich people were greedy from one of your parents, this would make you associate wealth with greed. This simple thought that had been enforced into your subconscious would prevent you from earning and holding onto any wealth. Your subconscious mind would have been conditioned, and the only way you would cope is to either make decisions which were bad, or let your money dwindle away.

Change your Verbal Programming

Being Aware - Write down all the statements you can remember relating to money that you heard as a child.

Understanding - Following on from this, write down how these statements have affected your current financial situation

Disassociation - Once you look at these you will see these thoughts are not yours, it is what you have come to believe by hearing them. Now you are in a position and have a choice to be different.

State your Declaration

All that I heard about money as a child might not be true. I choose a new way of thinking to support success and happiness.

Now touch your brow.

I possess the mind of a millionaire.

Chapter Four: The Four Elements and Luck

The Four Elements

We have seen there are four elements relating to change and which are crucial in allowing you to change your subconscious money map.

Awareness – unless you know of its existence, you are unable to change something.

Understanding – Once you come to understand where your thoughts and way of thinking originate, you see it has come from an external source and not from in yourself.

Disassociation – Now you understand these thoughts are not yours, you are in a position to spate yourself away from these ideas and to choose if it is worth keeping, or letting it go. These files of information you have stored may or may not have any information in them that is either truthful or of any value to the way you are now.

Reconditioning – Your declarations are one of the first steps in your reconditioning, and much more will follow once you see how wealthy successful people think. One by one these past thoughts you had heard can be changed to others that are more truthful and geared toward your goals.

Luck?

Before looking at the habits of the successful and the wealthy, we have to take a quick look at "Luck" and how it affects the outcomes. Generally speaking, luck plays no part in your success, unsuccessful people will say "they have not had much good luck, " or they are just not lucky.

It is true that you do need luck, yet there are four varying types of luck:

Random Good Luck

This is the sort of luck that we have no control over, this could be winning a lottery or being the beneficiary of an unknown inheritance.

Random Bad Luck

We have all had it at some stage, from becoming ill, a random accident or some other tragic event that like good luck, we have no control over.

Opportunity

Once we have good daily "Rich Habits," this type of luck becomes a byproduct. Once we plant those all-important "seeds" and we nurture the ever important "roots" we have this opportunity of the "fruits" that are bared. These fruits occur over the long-term rather than over the short-term. And as you should now see, rich people do things that benefit them over the long-term rather than a short hit.

Detrimental Luck

This is related to opportunity look, yet in a bad way. This is the luck that unsuccessful people encounter. They have bad habits, these of which are also grown from seeds (see mind map section) and have roots, these also bear fruits, yet these fruits are not the healthy kind. A loss of job, or making a wrong business decision can be related to this.

Once we understand everything relating to our mind map, we can follow our rich habits and the good fruits will be there for our picking. The laws of attraction come into play and the more we do in a healthy way, the more opportunity luck we will receive.

Chapter Five: Habits – Daily Habits and Goals

Habit One – Daily Habits

"I will create my good daily habits and follow these daily."

These are your foundation for success. Following on from earlier, we all have to become "aware" of our strengths and weaknesses and to do this we have to be completely, and sometimes brutally honest with ourselves.

Finding these traits can be difficult, we all have ego's that can get in the way and we have a level of uncertainty about our findings. It is easier for a third party to help with our assessment, that by doing it ourselves. An approach we can take in this self-assessment is look at our daily living patterns and habits. Once we recognize our everyday practices which are bad and holding us back, we will have taken another step toward our success.

On a sheet of plain paper create two columns, and in these list your daily bad habits, in the second column, you should write (invert) a daily practice that cancels out the bad daily habit.

Examples:

Bad Habit – I watch too much TV.

Good Habit – I'll limit myself to one hour TV per day.

Bad Habit – I don't return all my phone calls.

Good Habit – I'll return all of my phone calls in the same day.

There are many habits you can convert in this way, and once you have written all that you know. Follow your new good practices for one month. You should review these in the morning, noon and night so you can become accountable for following them. A good eighty percent of these should be completed on a daily basis.

Good Daily Habits Weekly Checklist (samples only)

I read for thirty minutes today on industry related materials.

I completed thirty minutes exercise.

I phoned one potential prospect today.

I wasted no time surfing the internet.

I told myself to do something "Today" when I did not want to do it.

I refrained from being sarcastic and saying something inappropriate today.

I followed my guidelines for my healthy diet.

I phoned one person just to say "Hi" or "Happy Birthday."

I completed 80% of my to-do list.

Conclusion

Successful people become slaves to their good daily habits, and they do this without finding it a chore, they relish and embrace this. **This is the first and most important "Rich Habit."**

Habit Two – Setting Goals

"I will set goals for each day, each month, each year and for the long-term. I'll focus on my goals each day."

To be successful, you have to be goal orientated, and these goals are created all the time. Your daily list of things to do represent your daily goals and your long-term goals list things that have to be completed at specific times.

Tip: Successful people think of work at work, and personal matters are left for outside the office.

Long-term thinking is a trait of successful people as they continually look into the future to see how they are performing against meeting their goals. The past is not dwelled on negatively, and any failures they encountered, they use as a way of learning how to do things differently.

Daily Goals

At the start of each day before doing anything relating to your business, plan your to-do-list or even better your desk planner and list the things that you have a high chance of completing. You will find that you can only achieve around 80% of what you have written. Times should be allocated for each assignment with the lower priority items being placed at the bottom of your planning.

Doing this can take away any frustrations you have by not completing your list. Once you have completed each task, mark it off as completed and then review your planner at the end of the day, and make yourself accountable for what you have achieved.

Monthly Goals

After your daily goals, you should list your monthly goals. As with your daily goals, you should list what has a high probability of being achieved. To make these more achievable, it is better to break these into steps, or way-points so you can see and accomplish these steps easier than trying to complete the whole task in one go.

Example:

If you are in the field of insurance policies and aim for writing a specific number during the month. You can break it down to calling or meeting a specific number of potential clients on a daily or weekly basis. This will come from the number of phone calls you have to make on a regular basis.

Yearly Goals and Objectives

As these are long term, it is not as easy to set yourself clear goals. These become more of a "wish list" of things to accomplish, and by breaking this down, you can create smaller goals on a monthly or weekly basis that will guide you toward reaching your yearly or long-term goals.

Example:

I wish to purchase a house within five years. To achieve this, I will save one thousand dollars per month for the next five years. To accomplish this, my expenses will be reduced, and this difference will be deposited along with my pay-check savings.

One way to keep track of your long-term goals is by creating a vision board, or a visual reminder of your objective. This can be a simple picture of the house that you wish to purchase, and by placing this in a visible place, it helps enforce what you are hoping to achieve.

Conclusion.

Successful people think for the long-term and set themselves goals. They also have a clear plan of how they are able to achieve their goals.

Chapter Six: Habits – Self-Improvement and Health

Habit Three – Self-Improvement

"I will fully engage and embrace self-improvement each and every day."

Successful people are always looking to improve themselves. Even if they fail, they take this as an opportunity to learn about how things don't work, and what to change for the better.

Industry publications and periodicals are often read on a daily basis to keep them up to speed on the aspects of their niche. Time spent surfing the internet or watching too much TV is not entertained.

Being a perpetual student can do nothing but good things. These successful people divide blocks of time that allows them to achieve this. Successful people know wasted time can be put to a much better use rather than spending it on something that is of no use to them.

All the successful self-improvement people follow becomes geared to achieving their desired goals. Either in the short term, but more often than not it used to achieve their long-term goals.

Self-improvement habits consist of something each day that improves your mind. This helps to expand your career or business even venturing into a new niche. Reading is most beneficial allowing you to become an expert in your chosen field. Rather than going forward with something you only know half information.

When your knowledge of a particular niche grows. You soon see opportunities present themselves rather than passing you by as you now identify the potential.

You should allocate times when you know you have no distractions. Either early in the morning before your regular workday or after your day is over. Whichever you choose you should set aside thirty minutes as at least for this activity. This short time may not appear to be much, yet accumulated over weeks and months it amasses to a large amount of time.

Conclusion

Successful and wealthy people devote time for self-improvement every day regardless of activities they have to perform.

Habit Four – Healthy Living

"Every day I'll devote time to my health in the form of exercise."

We all know how important health is, and that is in a regular person's life. Successful people make it a priority to assign time for this among everything else they do.

Not only considering and watching what they eat. Consumption is managed, and they perform regular daily exercise for a good thirty minutes. You also see successful people rarely overindulge in their food or their drink. If they do slip from time to time, they manage how they recover from this occurrence.

All of this exercise becomes a part of a wealthy person's routine, it is not something they perform when they have the time they make the time. This is one habit that is worth following closely, as exercise can improve brain function by quite a vast amount.

This routine exercise improves all of your immune system which in turn can result in fewer sick days over the course of a lifetime. Productivity can also be increased as a result as energy and stamina levels will rise.

Looking at the routines of successful people and how they take care of their health. Some have elaborate routines, or some have easy to follow routines. Each has their own, yet they support one that works for them to maintain good health and fit in with their workload.

I do not want to sound as if I'm preaching, or saying you should be on a diet, yet the easiest way to monitor your food consumption is by counting calories. This can seem like a chore, and to a certain extent, it is, in the beginning. As with anything in your niche you now see the benefits and eating to maintain your health is one more aspect of achieving your goals.

After a while, you will see what foods you can eat and what foods you can't. Once at this stage, it seems less of a chore counting calories. Now you will have, without realizing slipped into a much healthier eating pattern.

An effective weight management program allows you to have a few extra drinks or that second slice of pie. All it means is you understand the implications, and you offset this earlier in the day or at some other point.

As for exercise. The recommended minimum is thirty minutes of high activity cardio (anything that raises your heartbeat). This also helps to burn those extra calories you have consumed in the day.

Aerobics or other activities that raise the heartbeat are good examples. These are more effective than weight training or activities focusing on strength and stamina. These should be performed four or five days per week depending on your current fitness.

Simple tracking schedules can help you track eating and exercise habits. You now have the opportunity to use one of the many phone apps that do all this after a small amount of input from yourself.

Conclusion

Successful people plan their exercise and manage their consumption as they know a fit, and a healthy body equals a fit and healthy mind.

Chapter Seven: Habits – Relationships and Emotions

Habit Five - Relationships

"Each day I'll spend some time in forging more meaningful and lifelong relationships."

Relationships to wealthy people are like huge pots of gold. Have you ever noticed how many people they seem to know? These are not people who want something from these wealthy people, they are friends, longtime friends in most cases.

Although you might think that it seems a little overkill having this many friends, yet it is all done for a reason. Successful people nurture personal relationships, even business ones they often treat as personal.

Names, faces, birthdays and other snippets of information go a long way to make people feel wanted and most of all appreciated. The one thing that may appear strange is, successful people, do all of this even when there is nothing to gain from the other person. Yes, you read that right. There is no personal gain.

This is what we all call networking, and it is crucial for you to succeed. Many successful people develop a system that allows them to forge forward with their networking efforts.

There can be no end of reasons they seek out their contacts, a child's birthday, a wedding or even a phone call to congratulate a friend. They are all tools that help them increase their personal network and enforces their bond which in time turns into a lifelong relationship.

There are also likeminded people who successful people make a point of keeping in contact with. You will see successful people have no interest in forming a relationship with people who are only out for themselves. Ties to these people that are harmful or become destructive are cut at the earliest possible time.

In many cases, these people who have ties severed are in turmoil which is born out of a financial nature and are only out to seek assistance. These bad habits they possess can quickly drag another person down if they are not forceful and cut these ties.

Relationships are essential to successful people. They always return a phone call or look for other ways to improve their relations no matter how long it takes them. Many successful people use a system to remember all the information they can on their contacts. This can go far beyond name, telephone number, and address.

Any personal information deemed useful can be recorded. Spouse's names and birthday, their children's names, birthdays and schools, even down to what their children do as a hobby.

All of this can make contact feel as if they are your closest friend, in some cases, they might be. Yet when you are in a position to speak to them at this personal level, it will make them feel special and appreciated indeed.

A lot of successful people I have met over the years have admitted they are in fact not very good at remembering names. It is good to devise a system that can help you do this if you also have a problem.

There are many systems you can use for recording all of this information, and the one that works best for you is the one you should use. One word of advice, if you are attending an event, and you know who is going if you revise their information before you go. Your contact will feel special when you greet them by name.

Conclusion.

Successful people are not out to gain anything from their contacts. The sole aim is to increase their network. They make time each day to nurture their relationships and spend lots of time networking.

Habit Six – Relationships and Emotions

"Every day I'll control my thoughts and my emotions."

Successful people have a knack for being composed, and being able to keep their thoughts and emotions in check. It is rare for them to fall into a fit of anger, sadness, jealousy or any other harmful feelings. Any bad thoughts they have are cast out, and much of this thought pattern comes from the money map section.

If you have bad thoughts, you can make bad decisions which in turn create terrible consequences. Successful people are able to block out these bad ideas and replace them with good or positive thoughts.

When faced with a difficult situation, successful people can cope with this in a calm and organized manner as they use a technique.

First they **"Think"** followed by **"Evaluation"** and then they **"React."**

The first step gives them a chance to fully understand the situation. This, in turn, will provide them with more time to evaluate the situation. By this time they have had enough time to know the best course of action to take. Reacting is always the last thing they do as their action will more than likely be the correct action.

Sadness or depression are two other emotions successful people rarely become bothered with. They become engrossed in positive activities which divert their minds away from destructive emotions.

By filling your time with either projects or self-improvement. You will bolster your positive emotions, and block out harmful feelings that lead to a destructive nature.

Bad habits cause self-destructive attitudes. They occupy your mind when idle and are not involved in something that is constructive to achieve your goals.

If you find any of these types of emotion creeping in do something to occupy your mind. Either perform some self-improvement or go for a run or other exercise. This will prevent your mind filling with these thoughts.

Tip Exercise has been shown to reduce stress for up to twelve hours.

Conclusion

Successful people are fully aware of their thoughts and their emotions, they are also mindful of how they can block these from entering their mind.

Chapter Eight: Habits – Productivity and Rich Thinking

Habit Seven – Do it Now!!

"I will change my attitude too, 'do it now' and complete my list of tasks each day."

Procrastination is one thing that successful people never do. Putting things off becomes a bad habit and leads to a downward spiral of things that have to be done, and which never seem to get done. This leads to missed opportunities.

Many people use to-do lists, and as useful as they are, they don't help to plan your day. It is much better to use a desk planner that can show a full week at a time as well as the days in hours. With these, you can rank your tasks and allocate blocks of times against these throughout your day, and also see what is pending later in the week.

Successful people are driven by goals, yet it has been shown whatever's on your list of things to do, you will only achieve around eighty percent of this. It is for this reason you allocate time toward the end of the day for the least significant tasks.

When you spend the first part of your morning planning your day. You can decide if these tasks have become important enough to be done first, or they can be allocated to later in the day.

Successful people do complete things in a timely manner and never just let things fall by the wayside. They set goals and do everything they can to achieve these goals. Once you use a desk planner, you will fall into the "do it now" mindset that successful people have.

What you have on your list, you should aim to do without delay, and this goes for distractions and firefighting others problems.

If you find you have thoughts of putting things off. Repeat to yourself "I'll do it now" a few times. You can repeat them throughout the day, as this will reinforce it into your mind that everything has its time be completed.

There is one aside to this way of thinking, you become in control of your life, and you make the decisions rather than reacting to situations.

Conclusion

Successful people gain an "I'll do it now" attitude without a second thought of delaying their actions. This mindset opens many doors and opportunities for you.

Habit Eight – Rich Thinking

"I will change my attitude and spend time in rich thinking every day."

You will see that successful people have a positive attitude, they are energetic, well balanced and above all, they are happy with their lives. They are in control of their destination, confident and feel powerful.

These are reasons they become leaders rather than followers, and why so many individuals look up to them. All of these traits are not by accident or by luck, they have been tailored and created by their rich thinking habits.

Successful people like us all, will talk to themselves yet their words will never self-criticize, they will be uplifting and motivational. Congratulations are given to themselves when they reach an objective no matter how large or small.

Positive declarations are used (see money map section) as well as the ones who use positive affirmations. All of these reinforce an attitude, a successful attitude which helps to create that strong positive mindset.

If they encounter problems, they don't get down they see it as an opportunity, and if nothing comes of it, it was a learning experience, and it was never a failure. Bad thoughts become replaced with good thoughts as soon as they happen.

With all bad news in the world, it is not possible to block everything out. Successful people either keep away from overexposure to this sort of media, or they do something that is uplifting and beneficial.

The secret is in controlling what you see and hear every day and making sure that any negativity is balanced by something that is positive.

Successful people are also grateful, this in itself is a powerful tool, and can come in many forms, so much, so there have been books written on that very subject alone.

Declarations are mentioned in the money map section. These along with positive affirmations will reinforce a positive attitude into your mind if you do them as you should. These words we don't just feed our mind, they become lodged in our subconscious, and once they are there, we believe them without a second thought.

Declarations can be tailored to your situation, much as positive affirmations can be. Simple affirmations with a direct message work best. It is no good to be general with your affirmation as your mind will not understand what you mean.

Positive Affirmations

"I love my job."

"I am confident."

"I love working with others."

"I'm successful."

These are just a few examples, and there are much more as long as you are specific in what you wish to achieve. These give your mind a picture of the future you, the person you want to become. These should be written down, as this makes them more real and you should repeat them in the morning, lunchtime and in the evening to help reinforce the affirmation.

Conclusion

Rich thinking can help change your outlook, your mindset and your attitude amongst other things. You can quickly eradicate negative thoughts and replace them with positive, uplifting thoughts as soon as they occur.

Chapter Nine: Habits – Paying Yourself

Habit Nine – Pay Yourself First

"I will pay myself first, and save ten percent of my gross income from every paycheck."

When we have money, we always think we should settle bills and debts first. Although this is good, successful people always pay themselves first. This they do by taking ten percent from their paycheck and put it into savings or into investment, or even some fund that is linked to retirement.

Successful people invest wisely and watch over their savings while setting goals for returns on investments. You will find successful people have high credit scores and have a personal knowledge of their net worth. And they also keep an eye on their individual balance sheet.

When it comes to taxes, they use the best available financial professionals. These can maximize their returns and cut the amount of taxes they will pay.

Certified public accountants are the most trusted financial advisors and would be in the employ of a successful person, they might also seek assistance from certified financial planners and attorneys who specialize in estate or financial planning.

Retirement plans are also something successful people have, regardless of how much money they may have. This they would contribute as much as possible.

This goes for both self-employed and employed people who take full advantage of company retirement plans. The unsuccessful people concentrate on paying their credit cards, and other debts and bills and end up living paycheck to paycheck. Their financial situation is out of control, and they come to have bad credit scores as a result.

Many of these individuals also never make full use of a company retirement plan or have their own fund. They never take ten percent and put it in savings and then they are surprised when they come to retirement and are not in a position to fund their lifestyle.

Conclusion

Successful people pay themselves and save for their retirement, unsuccessful people forget to save and live paycheck to paycheck and work into their retirement years.

Chapter Ten: Mentors

All through the book, it has mentioned, we want to gain millionaires habits. As easy as it is to put all these changes in place and follow the practices, it becomes easier if we have a mentor whom we can model ourselves against.

We saw early on of the influences we had as a child and how they all affect our money map. How this affects our ability to become successful and wealthy is, we fear the worst will happen. We also tend to hang around with people who have negative attitudes (like attracts like).

A mentor will be full of good advice as they have already seen the problems and the pitfalls. As with your other relationships, these will be nurtured from both sides. This type of relationship can take time to develop, yet they should remain in place for many years to come. This has a two-fold effect, first is we forget names, and second, we become influenced by the people who are closest to us. As a result of all this, our subconscious makes us behave and think to the five closest people that we hang around with on a daily basis.

We are now led to the point, where we have to be careful and intentional whom we surround ourselves with.

Breaking away from this, and positioning yourself close to someone who has been there and done it already (your mentor), can be quite difficult. Two reasons being many people are unsure of whom to choose as a mentor, and second, they have no idea how to approach one.

Many successful people love to help other people, so once you have read the following steps of how to find one, and approach one. You will be well on your way. A good example is my father's friend who gave me that first bit of advice, which still resonates with me, and I have told that to many other people like you.

There may be a few of you who are wondering what a mentor is? To put it in simple terms:

A mentor is a person who can see that you have the ability and the talent within you, more than you might realize yourself. Once they know this, they can help you bring it out of you.

Step One: Who is my mentor?

Your mentor is a person who has been through all of what you are doing and is ahead of you by at least ten years. This mentor will represent whom you dream of becoming, and it will be a person you admire, respect and above all trust.

A mentor will be full of good advice as they have already seen the problems and the pitfalls, and as your other relationships, these will be nurtured from both sides as this type of relationship can take time to develop, yet they should remain in place for many years to come.

Step Two: Why do I need a Mentor?

This step is crucial for you to understand, if you do not know why it is essential to have a mentor, you will find you will fall short in other areas, namely your success.

Your mentor can bring a lot to the table as you can see from the following list:

A mentor helps to give guidance and direction and will help you take yourself to the next level.

Your mentor will help you to realize what your goals and dreams are.

A mentor has vast knowledge and expertise in business in general, not just in your niche.

Your mentor has had years of experience and has vast amounts of advice

Your mentor will help by offering support and can help you with your networking

A mentor can save you from many years of failure

A mentor will be able to see where you are going wrong and can help keep you on the right track

Once you build your relationship, you will be accountable to your mentor

Step Three: The places where to find a mentor?

A mentor can be found anywhere; you might even work or know someone whom you would love to have in this position. There are other places you can look if you do not know anyone:

Visiting industry events or trade shows

Motivational talks like conferences or seminars

The local chamber of commerce

A simple search in google, type in the name of a person you admire.

As you can see, a mentor can be found in many areas, yet it helps a lot if you understand the type of mentor you are seeking. This enables you to track them down much easier.

Step Four: Criteria when looking for a mentor.

This step is essential for you to understand, if you do not know why it is necessary to have a mentor, you will find you will fall short in other areas. Your mentor must see that you are serious about your business. As your possible mentor will already be successful, they will be managing their time, and as you know, things that are not of importance get pushed to the wayside. To assist here, make sure you are up to speed on your niche and your business, as they might ask many questions that they will expect answers to.

A mentor will also expect you to know quite a bit about their business. So before you approach them and make them the offer of a lifetime (to be your mentor), you should conduct some research about them and their business.

If you have not done your homework, a possible mentor will not take you seriously, and they know for sure that you are not willing to hustle for their experience and knowledge.

Step Five: Contacting your Mentor

Approaching a person and asking them to be your mentor can be the most challenging part. What I could quite easily say is, here is a script, alter it to fit your needs and send it off to your possible mentor.

That is not the best advice to give you at this point, the process of contacting a potential mentor will require a little more legwork on your behalf. If you are not prepared for them, they will not be ready for you.

There are five steps when approaching; parts you may have already started doing, but to keep things tidy, I will not assume you have begun.

Do your homework.

I mentioned researching your mentor, and I mean it. You should know them nearly as good as you know your own business. You have to go as far as, where have they come from? What are they doing now? How is their family situation? As well as finding their hobbies or favorite team, all of this shows you are interested in them as a person, and not just as a means to an end.

Explain why you are contacting them

After some substantial amounts of research, you are nearly ready to make contact. As you prepare this, you have to explain to your possible mentor the reason you are making contact in the first place. Many people hate to be bothered, successful people as much, if not more than a regular person.

If you give a valid reason why you are making contact, a possible mentor is more likely to take notice (you will not be the only one asking for assistance).

Reasons do not have to be complicated, as simple truths are better. Maybe you saw them at an event, so saying you wanted to introduce yourself, yet they were inundated with a crowd. You can also mention you both have shared friends, and one of them referred you to them?

No matter what the reason for contact, you stand more chance of a response if you give them a reason rather than plainly asking them to be your mentor.

Share Intentions and your desire for their assistance.

Once you have successfully made contact and your potential mentor has responded, you need to share with them your intentions. It is much better to inform them as early as you can of what you wish to gain from their input.

A quick email, phone call or a meeting can be enough for you to explain you are seeking a successful person who can be someone to give guidance or to just be someone who listens while you take your first steps to becoming successful.

The best way to move forward with this contact is by asking about them early in the conversation. First present your reasons followed by questions of how they are in life, and then ease into their business life. From here you can slowly move into your desires and your wish for them to become your mentor.

Your Goals

As you move further into a discussion of a possible mentorship, and they are warming to the idea of being assistance. You will have to inform them of your goals. Further discussion of the plan you have laid out for yourself to this point. Now also explain where you see yourself further into your professional career.

Mentor Schedule

Hopefully, at this point, you have a person who has agreed to be your mentor. Time is precious to both of you so you will have to add some formality to the proceedings. If you have decided on regular meetings, these should be planned in at a time that suits you both (more on the side of suits them). A monthly face to face meeting is ideal and gives structure to a mentor relationship.

In between these meetings, it is advisable to keep your mentor updated. An email giving updates is more often enough.

This structure is vital as, without it, you might find you are busy, and you both miss the chance to meet. When this happens, you can lose focus, and your goals are not reached.

How not to find a mentor.

Like yourself, a possible mentor is successful and busy. Above are ways of making contact and creating a relationship. Here are some things not to do while looking for a mentor.

Asking mentor upfront – being so abrupt will turn a possible mentor off the idea immediately.

Choosing a name rather than experience – as I mentioned, not all people are worthy of being mentors. You may feel a person is suitable as they are a CEO of a company, this assumption is wrong, and that person might never have had any experience in your niche.

Not Being Flexible – I mentioned a while ago that you have to set meetings that suit you both. If you reply "that time doesn't suit me" to a possible mentor, they will not be thrilled.

Asking questions that have answers on the Internet
– it is a waste of your time asking a question, and a possible mentor listening, where the answer is on the internet.

It is all about me – Mentors are inundated with requests all the time. If you make everything about you rather than having a two-way relationship, a mentor is more likely to pass you by and choose the one who has something to give back.

Lack of Gratitude – gratitude is a powerful tool as I mentioned. If a mentor is willing to help you, make sure you acknowledge what they are doing for you. Simply answering emails or returning calls, or even passing them your updates between meetings. All this shows you appreciate their help.

Conclusion

I would like to congratulate you on getting this far. Some of the principles mentioned in the book can take a little while to believe can be of use. Declarations and Affirmations come to mind immediately. In all honesty, though, these are not new ideas, they have been in use for many years.

As I mentioned, I was skeptical at first, about these and a couple of other of the principles, yet I followed what I had learned from my mentor (my father's friend) and after he had kept me in check and on the right path. I did succeed as I had mentioned.

It all comes down to re-conditioning your money map and your train of thought. If you disregard anything you have read, maybe having a millionaires mind and habits is not for you.

You have to want it, and you have to want it hard enough to believe in it, and you have to believe in yourself.

Now everything is down to you; you can start today. We know that leaving it until tomorrow is procrastination. Moreover, we know we cannot do that.

Don't leave something until tomorrow that you can do today. You do not have to have to start planning immediately or anything that takes up time, spend a few minutes thinking "rich" thinking and then do the following.

Put your hand on your heart (if you believe)

I'll start right now. I'll put my actions into motion.

Now touch your head. (And all say out loud together)

I possess a millionaires mind.

Printed in Great Britain
by Amazon